The NFL's Greatest Teams

# Seattle Seahawks

Marcia Zappa

Big Buddy Books
An Imprint of Abdo Publishing
www.abdopublishing.com

**www.abdopublishing.com**

Published by Abdo Publishing, a division of ABDO, PO Box 398166, Minneapolis, Minnesota 55439.
Copyright © 2015 by Abdo Consulting Group, Inc. International copyrights reserved in all countries. No part
of this book may be reproduced in any form without written permission from the publisher. Big Buddy Books™
is a trademark and logo of Abdo Publishing.

Printed in the United States of America, North Mankato, Minnesota.
092014
012015

THIS BOOK CONTAINS
RECYCLED MATERIALS

Cover Photo: ASSOCIATED PRESS.
Interior Photos: ASSOCIATED PRESS.

Coordinating Series Editor: Rochelle Baltzer
Contributing Editors: Megan M. Gunderson, Sarah Tieck
Graphic Design: Michelle Labatt

**Library of Congress Cataloging-in-Publication Data**

Zappa, Marcia, 1985-
  Seattle Seahawks / Marcia Zappa.
    pages cm. -- (The NFL's Greatest Teams)
  Audience: Age: 7-11.
  ISBN 978-1-62403-591-3
1. Seattle Seahawks (Football team)--History--Juvenile literature.  I. Title.
  GV956.S4Z37 2015
  796.332'6409797772--dc23
                    2014026444

# Contents

# A Winning Team

The Seattle Seahawks are a football team from Seattle, Washington. They have played in the National Football League (NFL) for more than 35 years.

The Seahawks have had good seasons and bad. But time and again, they've proven themselves. Let's see what makes the Seahawks one of the NFL's greatest teams.

Navy blue, green, and gray are the team's colors.

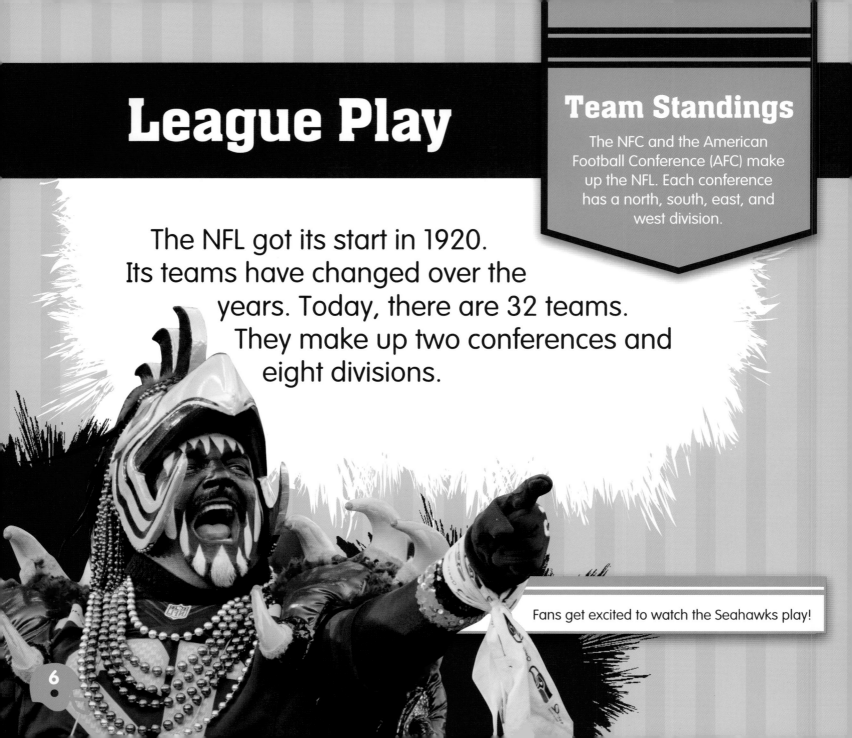

# League Play

## Team Standings

The NFC and the American Football Conference (AFC) make up the NFL. Each conference has a north, south, east, and west division.

The NFL got its start in 1920. Its teams have changed over the years. Today, there are 32 teams. They make up two conferences and eight divisions.

Fans get excited to watch the Seahawks play!

6

The Seahawks play in the West Division of the National Football Conference (NFC). This division also includes the Arizona Cardinals, the Saint Louis Rams, and the San Francisco 49ers.

The 49ers are a major rival of the Seahawks.

# Kicking Off

In 1972, the Seattle **Professional** Football group worked to bring an NFL team to the area. The group started building the Kingdome as a stadium for the team.

In 1974, the NFL agreed to let Seattle have a team. The Seattle Professional Football group held a contest to choose a team name. The Seahawks started playing during the 1976 season.

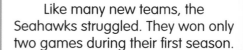

Like many new teams, the Seahawks struggled. They won only two games during their first season.

More than 1,700 different names were suggested in the team name contest. *Seahawk* is another name for an osprey. It was suggested 151 times in the contest!

# Highlight Reel

In 1977, the Seahawks moved from the NFC to the AFC. In 1978, they had their first winning season.

The team made it to the play-offs for the first time in 1983. They returned in 1984 and 1987. But after that, they didn't make it back to the play-offs until 1999.

## Win or Go Home

NFL teams play 16 regular season games each year. The teams with the best records are part of the play-off games. Play-off winners move on to the conference championships. Then, conference winners face off in the Super Bowl!

STEVE LARGENT
SEATTLE SEAHAW
1976 - 1989

Quarterback Jim Zorn (*left*) and wide receiver Steve Largent (*right*) were two of the team's early stars.

Jack Patera was the first coach of the Seahawks. In 1978, he was named the NFL's Coach of the Year.

The Seahawks returned to the NFC in 2002. They made it to the play-offs several times in the 2000s. In 2006, they went to the Super Bowl! But, they lost to the Pittsburgh Steelers 21–10.

In 2014, the team returned to the Super Bowl. Quarterback Russell Wilson led the offense. And, outside linebacker Malcolm Smith led the defense. The Seahawks beat the Denver Broncos 43–8!

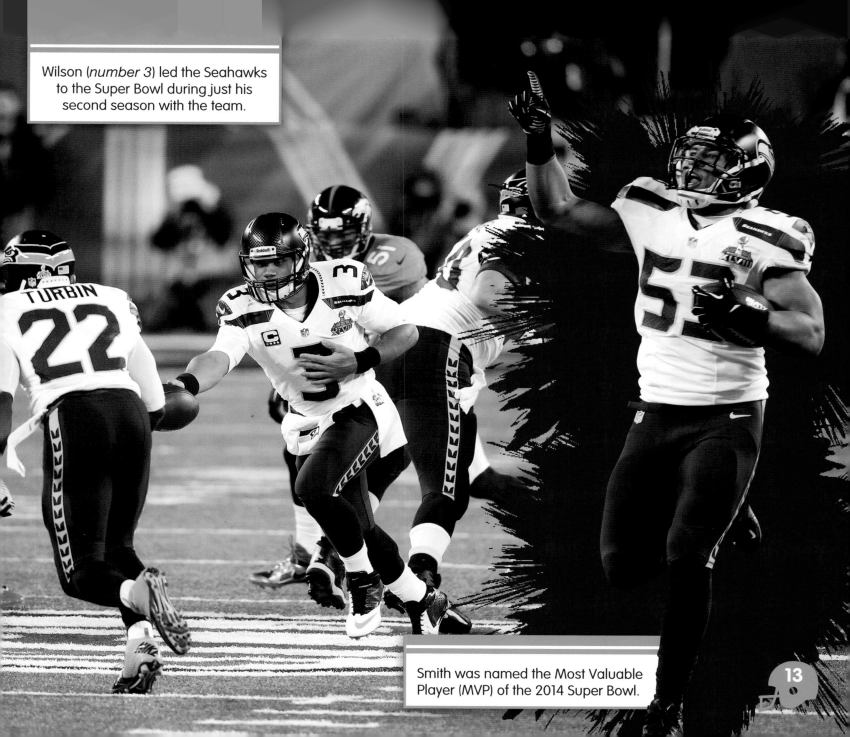

Wilson (*number 3*) led the Seahawks to the Super Bowl during just his second season with the team.

Smith was named the Most Valuable Player (MVP) of the 2014 Super Bowl.

# Halftime! Stat Break

## Team Records

**RUSHING YARDS**
Career: Shaun Alexander, 9,429 yards (2000–2007)
Single Season: Shaun Alexander, 1,880 yards (2005)
**PASSING YARDS**
Career: Matt Hasselbeck, 29,434 yards (2001–2010)
Single Season: Matt Hasselbeck, 3,966 yards (2007)
**RECEPTIONS**
Career: Steve Largent, 819 receptions (1976–1989)
Single Season: Bobby Engram, 94 receptions (2007)
**ALL-TIME LEADING SCORER**
Norm Johnson, 810 points, (1982–1990)

## Championships

**SUPER BOWL APPEARANCES:**
2006, 2014

**SUPER BOWL WINS:**
2014

## Famous Coaches

**Chuck Knox** (1983–1991)
**Mike Holmgren** (1999–2008)

## Pro Football Hall of Famers & Their Years with the Seahawks

**Walter Jones,** Tackle (1997–2008)
**Cortez Kennedy,** Defensive Tackle (1990–2000)
**Steve Largent,** Wide Receiver (1976–1989)

## Fan Fun

**STADIUM:** CenturyLink Field
**LOCATION:** Seattle, Washington
**MASCOT:** Blitz (*below*), Taima

# Coaches' Corner

Chuck Knox took over as head coach for the Seahawks in 1983. That year, he helped the team reach the play-offs for the first time. He led them to many more successful seasons.

Mike Holmgren became the head coach in 1999. He coached the Seahawks for ten seasons. That is longer than any other Seahawks coach. Holmgren led the team to the play-offs his first season. And, he led them to their first Super Bowl in 2006.

In 2010, Pete Carroll became the team's head coach.

After Knox left in 1991, the team won only two games. It was one of its worst seasons ever.

17

# Star Players

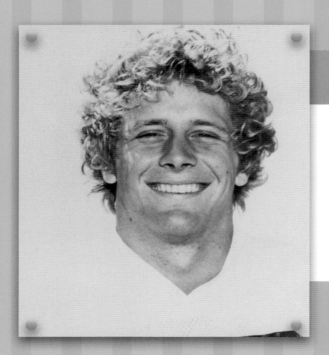

## Steve Largent  WIDE RECEIVER (1976–1989)

Steve Largent played for the Seahawks his whole **career**. When he **retired**, he held six NFL records. This included most receptions, most receiving yards, and most receiving touchdowns. In 1995, he became the first Seahawk in the Pro Football Hall of Fame.

## Kenny Easley  STRONG SAFETY (1981–1987)

Kenny Easley was the team's first pick in the 1981 **draft**. During his **rookie** year, Easley had three **interceptions** and returned one for a touchdown. In 1984, he was named the NFL's Defensive Player of the Year. Sadly, a sickness forced Easley to **retire** from the NFL after only seven seasons.

## Cortez Kennedy  DEFENSIVE TACKLE (1990–2000)

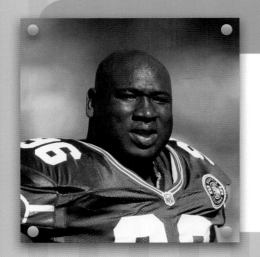

Cortez Kennedy was the team's first pick in the 1990 draft. He became a full-time starter in 1991. The next year, he had his best season, with 92 tackles and 14 sacks. He was named the NFL's Defensive Player of the Year. Kennedy was invited to play in the Pro Bowl, which is the NFL's all-star game, eight times.

## Walter Jones TACKLE (1997–2008)

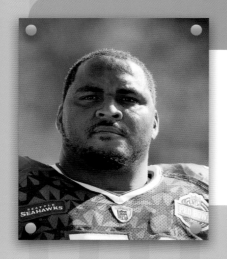

The Seahawks traded to get Walter Jones in the first round of the 1997 **draft**. He was an important part of the team's offensive line for 12 seasons. He played in the Pro Bowl nine times. That is more than any other Seahawk. And, he helped the team make it to its first Super Bowl.

## Shaun Alexander RUNNING BACK (2000–2007)

Shaun Alexander was known for his skill at running the ball and scoring touchdowns. In 2005, he scored 28 touchdowns in one season. At the time, this set an NFL record! Alexander became the first Seahawk named the NFL's MVP. He also helped lead the Seahawks to their first Super Bowl.

## Matt Hasselbeck QUARTERBACK (2001–2010)

Matt Hasselbeck led the team to the play-offs six times. And, he led the team to its first Super Bowl. When he **retired**, Hasselbeck had 29,434 passing yards. That is more than any other Seahawk.

## Russell Wilson QUARTERBACK (2012– )

As a **rookie**, Russell Wilson threw 26 touchdown passes. This tied the NFL record. He was named the Pepsi Max Rookie of the Year. The next season, he helped the team win its division. And in 2014, he led the Seahawks to their first Super Bowl win!

# CenturyLink Field

## Home Field Advantage

CenturyLink Field was built where Kingdome used to stand. It has a roof that covers many of the seats. But, the field is uncovered.

The Seahawks play home games at CenturyLink Field in Seattle. It opened in 2002. It can hold up to 67,000 people!

CenturyLink Field has a helmet wall called the "State of Football." It has model helmets from every high school football program in Washington!

23

# The 12th Man

**Earth Shakers**

Sometimes, the 12th Man is so loud, they shake the ground! The noise they make cheering has been recorded by local scientists as small earthquakes.

Seahawks fans are called the 12th Man. Football teams have 11 members on the field at a time. The fans are considered a twelfth member.

The 12th Man is known for being loud! The fans help the Seahawks by making it hard for the other team to hear. This can cause confusion and mistakes.

The team's **mascots** are Blitz and Taima. They help fans cheer on their team at home games.

Blitz the Seahawk has blue feathers. He wears jersey number 0.

Taima is an augur hawk. At home games, Taima flies ahead of the team and leads players onto the field.

Before every home game, the 12th Man flag is raised to honor Seahawks fans. Usually a local star or sports hero raises the flag.

# Final Call

The Seahawks have a long, rich history. They are known for their spirited fans. And in 2014, they became Super Bowl champions.

Even during losing seasons, true fans have stuck by them. Many believe the Seattle Seahawks will remain one of the greatest teams in the NFL.

The 12th Man holds a world record for the loudest noise made by a crowd at a sports stadium.

BOWL CHAMPIONS

27

# Through the Years

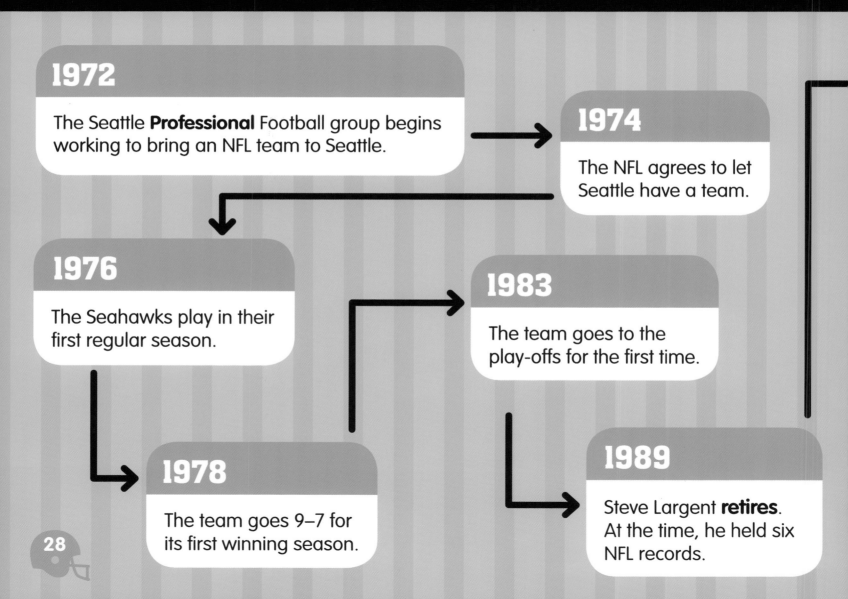

**1972**
The Seattle **Professional** Football group begins working to bring an NFL team to Seattle.

**1974**
The NFL agrees to let Seattle have a team.

**1976**
The Seahawks play in their first regular season.

**1983**
The team goes to the play-offs for the first time.

**1978**
The team goes 9–7 for its first winning season.

**1989**
Steve Largent **retires**. At the time, he held six NFL records.

28

## 1997

Businessman Paul Allen buys the Seahawks. He helps get the team a new stadium and stay in Seattle.

## 2002

Seahawks Stadium opens to replace Kingdome. Later, it is renamed CenturyLink Field.

## 2006

The team makes it to the Super Bowl for the first time.

## 2014

The Seahawks win the Super Bowl. They beat the Denver Broncos 43–8!

## 2012

The team goes **undefeated** at home.

# Postgame Recap

1. Who was the quarterback when the Seahawks won their first Super Bowl?
   **A**. Jim Zorn      **B**. Matt Hasselbeck      **C**. Russell Wilson

2. What is the name of the stadium where the Seahawks play home games?
   **A**. CenturyLink Field
   **B**. Seahawks Stadium
   **C**. Qwest Field

3. Name 1 of the 3 Seahawks in the Pro Football Hall of Fame.

4. How does the 12th Man help the Seahawks?
   **A**. They make a lot of noise, which helps confuse opposing teams.
   **B**. They help choose new players for the team.
   **C**. They practice against the team, which helps improve their skills.

1. C.   2. A.   3. See page 15   4. A.

# Glossary

**career** a period of time spent in a certain job.

**champion** the winner of a championship, which is a game, a match, or a race held to find a first-place winner.

**draft** a system for professional sports teams to choose new players. When a team drafts a player, they choose that player for their team.

**interception** (ihn-tuhr-SEHP-shuhn) when a player catches a pass that was meant for the other team's player.

**mascot** something to bring good luck and help cheer on a team.

**professional** (pruh-FEHSH-nuhl) paid to do a sport or activity.

**retire** to give up one's job.

**rookie** a first-year player in a professional sport.

**undefeated** not having any losses.

## Websites

To learn more about the NFL's Greatest Teams, visit **booklinks.abdopublishing.com**. These links are routinely monitored and updated to provide the most current information available.

# Index